# Start Being Productive NOW:

## The Real Deal
### of Being Productive in Life and Business

*Tyler Leap*

© 2016

## Essentials

If you really want to get wealthy, you have to become a creator. I want you to be a creator in your life. You have to be creating something of value in order to become rich.

What does it mean to be a creator? Are you a creator right now? This is an important question. Of course, the question goes even deeper into how much of a creator are you and what the hell are you creating with your time and your energy and your money.

People who are poor are really not creators. What they do is sell themselves out to an employer who then uses their services and you do work for the employer and you get paid X amount of dollars per hour, per month, per year, whatever the term is.

Therefore, sure, you could be creating stuff at your work. I'm not saying there is anything wrong with that. But you're not creating that much. You should be creating more. To become rich, you really need to create a lot, and you need to control the creation. This is critical. You need to control the creation.

Right now, for your boss, you probably are creating

stuff. Maybe you're creating reports. Maybe you're writing things. Maybe you're doing graphic design. Maybe you're creating engineering schematics, or you're providing some sort of organisation work as a secretary.

You're creating those reports, and organisation, and maybe you're managing people, but you're now owning it. The company owns it. The boss owns it. You're working for someone. It's really, really hard to become very wealthy, rich working for somebody else. Why?

Because they control the creation. They control the value. They put a glass ceiling on how much you can be earning, and how much value you could be generating for them. You might, right now, be stuck in a position where you are actually wanting to create more. You want to create more value for the company.

You want to do more for that project. You want to do more for your boss. This is very frustrating, because that boss or that company might not actually want you to be doing more. They might not be listening to your ideas. They might not be hearing your out.

Maybe you have a brilliant idea right now, that would earn millions of dollars for your company, but you're just in a position where you can't really exercise any creative control. You have no power of authority to get that idea pass through and realized. That value will never be generated. It will never be realized. You will then never see the payoff from that.

## Value Equals Wealth

Basically "wealth is value".
The more value you can generate for the world and other people, the more wealth you will generate for yourself. It comes back to you. This is a very tried and true principle. What you've got to do is position yourself to create more value for the world.

What does that mean? For you, it might mean put out more novels, put out more writing. Put out more blog posts. Put out more engineering schematics if you're an engineer. Put out more computer code if you're a computer programmer.

You have to be smart about this. That doesn't mean work harder on your job. In fact, I think that can be a dangerous trap to fall into, to think that "If only I just worked harder on my current job, I would become rich."

Actually, you probably wouldn't. You might get promotions, and certain jobs offer so much room for growth that you actually could become very rich just working in your company and working your way up the corporate ladder.

That tends to be pretty rare. I actually find that the best way to become rich is to start owning the creation. To do that, you generally need to become a partner, a shareholder, a stakeholder in some way, or you have to start your own business.

I really recommend the last option, starting your own business. Don't let that discourage you from generating wealth for yourself, even in your current job. I'm not saying quit your job today or you're never going to be wealthy.

I'm just saying think down the road. Be smart about this. If you recognize that right now, you're not able to have the kind of creative output you would want, you're not able to create massive value, then start to think what you can do to change that.

One of the things might be to start looking for either a new job, where you can really express yourself, share your gifts more, or create your own job, create your own business. Start fleshing out those ideas.

## Create Something

This idea of being a creator — you have to be creating something. Create something. What does this really mean? For most of you, there are two things here. One is put yourself in a position where you actually can be fully expressive.

The next point is that, for many of you, you are probably not creating anything in your life right now, at all. Many of you be going to a nine-to-five job where you're doing some piddly type work for an organisation whose value you don't really believe in, whose mission you don't believe in, whose products you don't believe in, you don't really care about.

You're not really putting any passion into it and if you're in that position, I do not consider you a creator. Even if you're creating stuff for the company you're not really a creator. A creator is someone who has vision. Someone who puts their blood and sweat into their work. They take their work very personally and they care not about the paycheck, and not company loyalty or making sure they don't upset their boss or something silly like that.

What they care about is creating something beautiful and excellent for humanity, for the world. They want to put stuff out. That's all a creator cares about. A creator, this is not some magical unicorn type of person, this is not some mystical fairy tale creature. A creator is just someone who has put a lot of value on this.

Some people come about this very naturally, through the way they're raised. Other people, maybe like you right now, don't see themselves as a creator. You can refashion yourself into a creator, and when you do... wow. You're going to have some amazing things happen.

First thing that's going to happen is you're actually going to enjoy what you're doing at work. The next thing that's going to happen is that you're actually going to get excited waking up in the morning. You're going to have so much more drive and passion. People are going to see that on you.

The next thing is going to actually position you to be extremely rich. You can't get rich by doing ordinary work, not really. If you're extremely lucky maybe you can, but you can't really get rich in this world by doing mediocre work. You have to do extraordinary work. You have to be exceptional.

## Create Purple Cows

As Seth Godin puts it, you have to be creating purple cows. You have to be creating things, projects or services that are remarkable. It has to be remarkable. What are you doing, what are you creating that is remarkable? If you're not creating anything remarkable, then you're never going to be rich. That is the bottom line.

A couple of other points — I've kind of beat this creator one to death. The next point I'm going to say is that a lot of you right now are probably saying "Yes, I want to be a creator. This is actually something I've been really passionate about. I've wanted to be a creator my whole life. I've been thinking about it but I'm just stuck. I'm stuck. Things are not letting me be a creator. My parents are holding me back. My friends are holding me back. My boss is holding me back. My company is holding me back.

People don't see my potential. People don't see what I can do for them. My money situation is holding me back. I don't have enough capital. I don't have enough capital to start a business. I don't have enough money to take some time off to define my life purpose or to look for a new job. I don't have that luxury."

## Take Responsibility

Here's the deal. This is the biggest thing actually, even bigger than being a creator, that is holding you back from being rich. You're not rich because you're blaming other people. You're not taking responsibility for your life and the circumstances that you're in. You're not doing it.

What's even worse is that you're going to deny you're a victim, you're making yourself a victim, you're going to deny this. You're going to blame me for telling you and accusing you of being a victim. You're going to say to yourself "No, these are real problems I have in my life. This is tangible. I don't have money. My mom is really holding me back. My dad is really holding me back. My spouse is really holding me back. My boss is a total donkey, has no vision, doesn't see my potential."

You're going to say all of that is true for you and that I'm wrong. I'm not wrong. I'm right and you're wrong. Right now, you're putting yourself in such a victim position that you're not even realising what you're doing.

Here's what's going to happen: you can either be a victim and stay a victim in your life and keep getting the kind of results that you've been getting, or you can open your mind up and accept these new ideas and let your ego get bruised by the fact that you are sabotaging your own life. Start making the hard changes you have to make to start to get a transformation.

In this case, becoming rich. Your boss is not really holding you back. What's holding you back is your thought that your boss is holding you back. Your parents aren't really holding you back. What's holding you back is your thought that your parents are holding you back. It's the assumptions you have.

It's the assumptions you have about what you need to move forward. I don't have enough money. How can I move forward? My parents are so negative and controlling and dominating, and the way they raised me. How can I possibly move forward?

My health is bad, I don't feel good. Maybe I have some illness. How can I possible move forward from that? These are real, physical, tangible things. My boss, he really won't let me get promoted. He doesn't want to hear my ideas. How can I get past that?

I hear what you're saying and I know exactly how it feels. I feel this way at times, and I've definitely been there. But this is the biggest thing that's holding you back from creating wealth, from being rich and getting success in any area of your life.

## Don't Let The Outside Control You

It's holding you back so much, because what you're doing is giving your power away to all these external circumstances. You're being mesmerised by your external circumstances.

What's happening right now is that you're limiting your options because you think you're stuck, and you've got these assumptions. Really, what you're doing is thinking inside a very small, confined little box. That little box is keeping you where you're at. It's keeping you kind of comfortable, but also very frustrated.

What you've got to do is expand that idea. You've got to expand it, and the way to do that is to say "OK, from now on, no more complaining.

No more negative thinking. No more finger pointing. I am responsible, one hundred percent, for my whole life, for everything."

I mean everything that happens to you. I don't just mean when you cut somebody off on your way to work because you're so rushed, and then that person flicks you off. You're not just responsible for that. You're obviously responsible for that.

I mean you're responsible for everything. You are responsible for your boss being an ****, and not listening to you. You are responsible for your parents having a negative impact on your life and holding you back. You are responsible for where you're living. You're responsible for how much you're earning, your responsible for your health. You're responsible for everything.

You don't want to hear this, I know you don't. It's very threatening to your ego. You know what's also awesome, though? What's awesome is that when you accept this, what this means is that you have complete power to change everything in your life. And that my friends, is true. That is very true.

That is what you've been denying yourself. When you create this victim mentality, when you cast yourself as the victim, what that means is that you can stay a victim. There is a psychological payoff that you get from being a victim, which is "Look at me, I'm a victim, I can't do anything. I don't have to go out there and work my ass off to change."

When you accept responsibility for everything, all of a sudden the whole world opens up to you. Everything is possible. Now you see opportunities, and you see things you can do. You see the really scary thing, this is why you don't want to take responsibility for your life. You see the scary thing, which is so  scary. The reason you're not more successful is because of you. It's because you're afraid of your own potential. That is the real truth of why you won't take responsibility for your life. You are afraid of what you will take of you, to work, to live into your full potential.

## It's All About Marketing

I'm gonna give you more practical, more quick to implement type of ideas. I think the biggest idea that you need to understand to make more money is you need to start to learn marketing. You need to understand the principles behind marketing. Because marketing is all about how to sell something or convince someone of the value of what you have to offer. And marketing is much broader than we initially think it is.

Marketing will tell you how to sell yourself to a company, how to sell yourself to an employer, how to sell yourself to a client, how to attract more business, how to even build up a charity and get attention to your charity, even if a non-profit. How to attract the opposite sex, because that also involves using the principles of marketing.

Marketing is very important, and what marketing is gonna teach you if you start learning it is that you need to provide value. You need to understand what the other person wants, and what is valuable to the other person. Then you can tailor a proposition that will appeal to them.

If you're only thinking about yourself, and you're thinking about how to leech value from your employer, or you're thinking about how to leech the most value from your clients and your customers, or a relationship – I hope you're not doing that in a relationship – then what's gonna happen is that it's gonna come back to bite you in the but.

## Providing value

Naively, it seems like "Well, let's try to leech as much value and we're gonna get the most money", right? It doesn't work that way. What I find works much, much better, and what all the self-help gurus out there, all the people that have come before me who have studied this stuff, and have really made big successes of their lives, all come to the consensus that you need to be providing value.

What does that mean? That means, for example, if you're working at a company, and right now you're in a kind of a mid-level position – like a salesman, an engineer, or an accountant, whatever – and you wanna make more money and within that same organisation, then what you gotta do is provide more value to the company. You wanna provide it in a way where it's obvious to them, and you wanna provide it in a context that they actually want and need.

For example, you might go to your boss, and you might ask them: "What are you guys working on next? What's the next big thing? How can I contribute the most? Let's say I really wanted to develop myself, and I wanted to build skills and I could give you guys the most value, what would that look like, for you guys? If I actually went and made all those changes, what would that be worth to you guys? Would you be willing to give me a promotion? Would you be able to give me a pay bump? Would I get a bonus? What could I get? Could I get some perks, some more vacation time?"

## Hunting For Opportunities

This is how you do it. You gotta look at where the opportunities are within your company. What are they doing next? What is gonna earn them more money? Whatever earns them more money, they can then justify paying you more for. Because if you could earn your company an extra hundred thousand dollars a year with what you're doing, either a programme that you're writing, or the sales that you're making, or the customers you're attracting, or the advertising you're putting out there.

If that's giving them a hundred thousand dollars cash, and they can see that clearly, link that to your efforts, then they can understand it's just viable to pay you some percentage of that. They can justify paying you probably as much as half of that, but more likely they're gonna give you ten percent of that, or twenty percent. It all depends on your situation.

Look for value. If you're running your own business, and you wanna make more money that's almost easier. What you gotta do is go and ask your clients, interview your clients and get a deep understanding of what your clients want. What are their real needs, not what you think they want, but what do they say they really want. Then tailor your services to really provide that to them.

Provide what they want more of, and they're gonna pay you for it, appropriately. Go ahead and ask them. Most entrepreneurs and business leaders actually don't have a very crystal clear understanding of exactly what it is their clients and their customers want, cause they never sat down and went through that process of finding out. That can be a process that requires some work. If you do that, you're gonna increase the amount of compensation you're getting. You're gonna increase the amount of money you're charging.

## Asking For More

Other ways to make more money? Well, simply ask for it. That's a simple one, have you tried that? How many people have actually asked for more money? A lot of times we have hesitation, we feel like we don't deserve it or we feel like if we ask something bad is gonna happen and we're gonna get rejected or fired, or the client's gonna leave us.

Well, in a lot of cases, you're undercharging for your services or your products. Whether you're working at a company, or you're running a business and selling your own services and products. You can usually charge more. A lot of times, you can charge double more, and you'd be surprised to find that clients and customers and employers will pay for it.

It all depends on what your positioning is. You should at least try. Do you go in and ask for a yearly salary bump? Do you at least try to do that? Maybe ask for a ten percent raise every year. Make it a habit of doing it. Maybe ask for twenty percent raise. The more you ask, the more you try for it, the more likely you are to get it. If you never ask for raises, no one's gonna come to you and just hand you a raise.

It's the same thing with your clients. See if you can charge them more, raise your prices by ten percent, raise your prices by twenty percent, see what happens. You might be surprised at just how much free money you're losing right now because you're too hesitant and you're limiting yourself in your mind, basically, as to how much you can charge.

If your clients are getting a lot of value from what you're offering, and they don't have a lot of other options to go to, and you're not in a super competitive business, then you can probably charge more for what you're doing.

## Sell Your Uniqueness

Which leads me to the last point, which I think I'll talk about here, which is a more fundamental principle about how to earn more money in whatever it is you're doing. That is to position yourself into a place where you're providing something unique that other people are not providing.

The problem with selling a commodity, like if you're selling gasoline, wheat, or bubble gum is that this stuff is – these markets are so competitive that prices are pretty much set. You can't really charge much more for bubble gum than what it costs. You can't really charge much more for gasoline or for wheat than the market price. There's an industry price.

If you're providing some sort of unique product, some sort of unique service, something you have patented, something that you're doing for a company that no-one else can do, then you have some leverage. Now, all of a sudden, you can charge more. It is about creating more leverage in either your business or your career.

In your career, the way you create leverage is becoming very, very good at it. Becoming so good that nobody else is as good as you, and nobody can deliver the same kind of results and value as you. For example, if you're working for a company as their advertising guy then the better you can market, the more tricks and techniques you know, the more connections you have built with other marketers in the industry, and the more you can leverage them, then the more value you're able to provide.

It's a simple math calculation. If you can provide a million dollars worth of value to somebody, then they're gonna be willing to pay you at least ten percent of that. You're at least worth ten percent.

## Building Up A Brand

If you can provide a million dollar worth of value, they'll give you at least a hundred thousand. Maybe more, depending how good you are at negotiating. The same is with your business. What are you providing that's unique about your business? How are you setting up your business that you're offering a unique selling proposition? How is your product so unique that even if you charge a little bit more for it, customers would still want it?

That usually means building up a brand. That usually means building up some unique points, some unique features that will keep customers coming to you, even though there are other people out there. Maybe your product quality is exceptionally high. Maybe your service quality is exceptionally high. Whatever that is, maybe you just have amazing branding, and you're the top of the industry, you're the industry leader in your niche.

That will allow you to charge more money, and any kind of actions you can use to build up and elevate any one of those pillars I just mentioned will allow you to charge more money. I think the ultimate strategy here is to make yourself unique. To do that, that means putting in the hard work and the time it takes to build it up.

It doesn't matter if you're building up a brand for your company and you're investing time and money into building up that brand over a span of a decade. Or you're doing that with your career, and you're building up yourself as a brand, as someone who's an expert in your own industry, whatever industry that is.

If you're a florist, make your self a world-class florist. If you're an athlete, make yourself a really world-class athlete. If you're an engineer, become a really talented, accomplished engineer, with patents behind you. Something like that will make you much more marketable.

## Spreading The Word

The final thing that I'll probably end on is – I already mentioned a little bit of this building up your expertise, but also building up your renown in your industry. Getting a little bit of fame. I don't mean like celebrity fame, although that can be lucrative in and of itself, but for most of us it's not about fame, it's about building up a certain authority and expertise.

Like I said, within your industry, are you well known? Do you have articles published under your name, in your industry, as an expert? You don't? Why not? Are you going to all the conventions and the industry events? Are you in touch with the leaders in your industry? Are you friend with them? Are you acquaintances with them? Are you in a mastermind group with them?

All of those things will raise your value. First of all, you'll learn so much more. Second of all, you'll have more options, you'll have connections. It's really powerful to have connections. It's really powerful to have your name out there. Once you have a little bit of a reputation, even if it's just within your narrow little niche, then what happens is that your market value skyrockets. And it doesn't skyrocket proportional to the value you give, it skyrockets much more.

When people recognize you – think about that, if you go into a job interview, and you go in, and there's you who has ten articles published, maybe a blog that people in this industry follow. Then there's the other guy, who just has a normal, vanilla resume, and maybe has ten, or even twenty years of experience, but he doesn't have any sort of image out there, no personal brand built up.

Who do you think they're gonna hire? Who do you think they're gonna pay more? You, by a big, big margin. So go ahead and start building that up for yourself. Create a strategy for how you're gonna do this. Do that for your business, do that for the brand of your business, and if you're just a career professional, do it for your career. Super, super important. With career it usually means building up connections and training. Getting lots and lots of training, and lots and lots of practice, until you're really, really good.

# How To Become a Millionaire

## The Proper Principles

I don't know if you've looked around, but the majority of people are not millionaires. That is not because of luck. That is not because they weren't born into the right family. That is not because they don't have the right connections. That is because they're not following the proper principles for how to become a millionaire.

When you start to get these in line and you go out and work them — you have to work them, there's no magic pill, you have to work them really hard — when you know the principles and your work them really hard, then your chances of becoming a millionaire increase exponentially.

It's pretty much guaranteed that if you want to become a millionaire, and you really work towards it, you will become one in your lifetime. Let's talk about how to actually do it. Not the nonsense, the real principles involved.

First of all, the first principle is that there are no secrets. There are no shortcuts. There are no gimmicks. Luck is not a factor. A millionaire is someone who is a boss. By boss, I mean not just an employer of people, but a boss in the sense of he or she has power, has authority over themselves.

They are in control. A millionaire is control of his own mind. He does not buy into this idea that somehow, by luck, he's going to become wealthy and successful. Definitely not. If you're coming from that mindset that's pretty much an end to it right there. That guarantees you will never become a millionaire.

Even if you do, by a fluke of luck, you're going to lose all that money anyway. It's going to be of no value to you. To become a millionaire, what you need to do is really be serious with yourself. How wealthy are you right now?

If you're coming from a middle class background, or a lower middle class background, or even poverty, if you're coming from a place where millions of dollars seem like "Oh my god, that's amazing. It's impossible to even dream of that. That would be a dream come true." — if you're coming from that kind of place, then here's what you're going to need:

You're going to need radical self-growth, to become a millionaire. This is what's going to be required. I'm going to talk about some business aspects later in this book. This book is not just about personal growth. Personal growth is the core of it.

The reason you're not a millionaire, and the reason you're never going to become a millionaire, doing what you're doing right now, is because, basically, you're not resourceful enough. Your psychology is not going to permit you to do it.

You have too many limiting beliefs. You have too much social conditioning. You have a groove you've set yourself in, financially and in other ways. Basically, you're going to run along in that groove and — to become a millionaire, let's face it, if you're earning let's say fifty thousand dollars a year right now, which is kind of an average salary, or even if you're earning a hundred thousand dollars a year.

That's nice, but if you're in that place, then that's ten to twenty-fold increase you need just to reach a million dollars. That's not going to happen through just a series of promotions. You're not just going to get promoted and become a millionaire one day. Almost guaranteed that's not going to happen.

To reach the status of millionaire, you need to reach millions of dollars. To reach millions of dollars, you need to start doing something radically different in your life. To be able to do something radically different in your life, that means you need to be able to do something radically different in your life.

Most people can't do that, because their psychology won't permit them. It's their mindsets. It's not even so much about the work they're doing out in the world. A millionaire does the same kind of work that a non-millionaire does, except that a millionaire has a whole different slew of mindsets and habits and practices that are completely night and day from what the average person is doing with their life.

## Take The Reins

First of all, I want you to completely forget about outer circumstances. I want you to completely forget about the economy, the lack of money you currently have, luck, any lack of education you have, any lack of social status or social connections, any limitations you might feel from your family or the country you grew up in, or the bad boss you have, or the marriage you're in, or the relationship that's holding you back, or that bad childhood event you had — all of that has to go.

You cannot be a victim and be a millionaire at the same time. You have to choose one or the other. Most people are not millionaires simply for this reason, because they cast themselves as victims. They don't take full responsibility.

You need to take full and utter responsibility for absolutely everything in your life, not just money, but especially money, especially career and especially business. Those are what's actually going to create millions of dollars.

You need to take responsibility for the other aspects as well. You need to take responsibility for all your negative thoughts, for all your neurotic behaviour, for all the ways in which you get angry and upset and fearful — you can't keep those as excuses.

You have to work on every one of those parts of your life in order to raise yourself up, to earn millions of dollars in a sustainable way. You're going to have to work really hard on yourself. This is where people make a mistake — they think they're going to work really hard on their job, they're going to work really hard on their career, and then that's going to produce millions of dollars.

The problems is that most people can work 'till they're blue in their face on their career, for decades, and they'll still never be millionaires. The reason is not because their career doesn't have the potential to earn them millions of dollars. It actually does.

Most careers, if you structure them properly and you come at them with the right thinking, can produce millions of dollars. Except, most people are not equipped with the mindset they need in order to capitalize on that. They're never going to actually go out there and do it.

## Work Better, Not Harder

Working at your job harder is not how you become a millionaire. That's a trap. I'm not saying you should quit your job right now. I'm not saying you should slack off at your job. I'm not saying you shouldn't study and be better at your job, and do it excellently. You should.

Just realize, to become a millionaire, it's going to take a lot more. It's the mindsets. Here's the thing: you have a thermostat in your brain that actually has a set point for what you're earning per year. It's not the external circumstances. It's the inside, here you have this little subconscious thermostat level, which has you pegged somewhere.

It's got you pegged at twenty thousand a year, fifty thousand a year, seventy thousand a year, a hundred thousand — whatever it is that you're making. You have to assume you're going to stay at that level. If you want to shift that thermostat, you're going to have to do some internal work.

Stuff is going to have to happen. Radical stuff. You can't get from fifty thousand a year to a million a year. That's not going to happen if you don't be serious with yourself and tell yourself that something really major has to change with your life. It's got to change on the inside first.

What you've got to start to understand is that millionaires have a different mindset and a different philosophy. They take philosophy seriously. They take their mindsets very seriously. They take their own personal growth very seriously.

What they do is fundamentally work on themselves, to make themselves more resourceful, so that they can go and create value for the world. A millionaire is going to value education. He's going to be a lifelong learner. Critical for being a self-made millionaire.

## Have The Right Beliefs

Beliefs: a millionaire is going to have very healthy, empowering beliefs about money, about success, about his own ability to control circumstances around him. He has to feel empowered. You can't just go out there and create an extraordinary business, or generate some sort of product, or do something good for the world that's going to generate a lot of value and bring you money back in return.

You can't do that if you feel like you're a victim and you have no control. You need to start to work on your beliefs. If you have beliefs around scarcity, lack of money, how money is evil, how corporations and businesses are evil, how the only people that are rich are the ones that scammed others and have done something nefarious — if you have these kinds of mindsets, then you're basically fucked.

You're never going to become a millionaire because you're so stuck in your limiting beliefs that you simply can't. Could you imagine being a millionaire and thinking all those things? It would be so incompatible. Your self-image would be so incompatible with your external circumstances that there would be just complete discord.

You would drive yourself nuts. Something catastrophic would happen. You would lose all that money. Your subconscious mind would sabotage you in such a way that you would lose that money because it would be too painful to hold onto it while you're preserving these beliefs.

Something has to go. Either the beliefs have to go, or you are going to stay where you're at, but you're not going to have the millions of dollars. Personally, I would much rather have millions of dollars than hold on to poor beliefs. I do everything I can to eradicate every single last strand of negative limiting belief I have in myself.

I work very hard to do that, because I know that I need to, to become a millionaire. We already talked about millionaires having to take responsibility, so that's very important. But a millionaire also has to have purpose. We're not just making you a millionaire just so that you have money. That's not how a millionaire gets made.

A self-made millionaire doesn't become a self-made millionaire just because he's chasing after money. That's not a valid motive, not a valid reason. Usually millionaires and entrepreneurs are actually very focused on the world. They're focused on what they can do for the world. They have some sort of drive, some sort of passion.

There's something they love to do, and there's some way in which they love to influence the world. As a millionaire, as a business owner, if you have a popular or successful career, that gives you authority. That gives you impact. You should use that for some sort of greater good.

The reason you should do that is not simply because you're helping the world, although it's a nice reason, but because it's going to motivate you. To become a millionaire, you have to work your ass off. You're going to work harder than you've ever worked in your life.

Not just on the externals, and on your business, but also on the inside. You're going to have to work really hard on the inside. To have the motivation and the perseverance to do that, to have the willpower to go through that whole journey of massive self-growth you're going to have a deeper purpose.

Money is not going to be sufficient. Money's never going to motivate you enough to do all that. Life purpose, very important.

## Think Critically

The last point I would make about philosophy is that a millionaire is very independent-minded. He cannot be hemmed in by what the market tells him. He cannot be hemmed in by what his family tells him. He cannot be hemmed in by what society is telling him, by what the economy is telling him.

A millionaire has to bust through that, because the obstacles to create a business that will earn you that much money is going to require you to be an independent, critical thinker, be a bit of a maverick and a rebel. That's also part of the philosophy of being a millionaire.

You have to start to embrace that. Stop relying on other people to give you answers, give you easy answers. Stop looking for easy stuff. A millionaire goes out there and he embraces the challenge of it. He thinks for himself.

## How To Actually Get There

What does it actually take, on a practical level, to start to earn lots and lots of money? This is not some airy-fairy notion, this is very concrete. You need to have seven digits in your bank account. How do you get there?

This goes back to the fact that you can't really get there by just working harder at your current job. If you're working a nine-to-five job, very few nine-to-five jobs will allow you to rise to millionaire status. Only if you rise to a CEO position, or some sort of very high-level management position within a large corporation can you be earning that kind of money.

The other option then is to become self-employed. That's basically what you have to do. You have to become an entrepreneur, a business owner or become self-employed. There's different classes of millionaires out in the world. Some millionaires start businesses.

They start corporations. It could be a small corporation of five people. It could be a larger corporation of twenty people, a hundred people, tens of thousands of people. There's a whole spectrum, and you could be earning millions of dollars anywhere along that scale of sizes.

That's not the only way to become a millionaire. You can become a millionaire just being a one-man shop. This is what a lot of celebrities do. This is what a lot of artists, musicians do, bloggers, people who own internet businesses.

A lot of these types of businesses these days can be one-man shops, where you basically do everything, and then you maybe outsource certain things to other people, you have a couple of assistants may be helping you. Basically, your business is you, especially with someone like a celebrity or an athlete.

They're making a business out of their life. In that case, you can make a lot of money doing that. In fact, celebrities are some of the most highly paid people in the world, compared to, let's say, a CEO.

Most CEOs will never match the kind of money a celebrity will pull in, or the kind of money a really big athlete or musician will pull in. That's also a very valid path. You can become an author, you can become a celebrity, a musician. If you're more artistic, those things can work really well for you.

## Work For Yourself

Either way, you have to become self-employed. It's not going to work, staying at your job. This is another reason why most people will never become millionaires. They are too afraid to leave their job, and they're to afraid to face the risk of not having money to pay the bills.

It is challenging. This is something I went through. I'm self-employed and financially independent now, but it is a real challenge to make that transition, from having a stable nine-to-five career to working for yourself and having to worry about all that stuff yourself.

What a lot of people don't realise, when they're working in a corporate job, they don't realise how much of the really challenging stuff is being done by the leaders of the organisation, or how much of it has already been done decades and decades ago, by the original founders.

Now, they're just kind of coasting on the company success and just typing away at their computer, and they can expect to get a paycheck. When you become self-employed, you quickly realize that it doesn't work that way. When you're self-employed, it's all about value. How much value can you give the other person?

You're going to have to start to worry about value. You're going to have to start to worry about legal issues, marketing issues, logistical problems, employment problems. All these sorts of business issues, all of them come into play. You have to worry about economics and paychecks. It's quite a lot to take on.

That's stuff you have to worry about on top of whatever work you're doing. That's all added on top of the workload you've already got. It can be really challenging to go through that stuff. That's why most people will never do it.

The upside is that if you do do it, then you can position yourself very nicely to be earning a lot more than you would have if you had been working at that nine-to-five. Right now, if you're working a nine-to-five, and you have a dream of becoming a millionaire, you have to start asking yourself "How do I make the transition?"

Start to look for different strategies and techniques that you can use, opportunities you can use to start to move yourself out of that. That's a very interesting and fascinating topic, and I'll share my own experiences with how I did that, the pros and cons and various approaches for how to do that. You have to start keeping an eye out for it. Your nine-to-five is not going to do it.

## Generate Value

The last principle I'm going to give you is the idea that you need to be generating lots of value in the marketplace to be earning lots of money. You're not going to become a millionaire by doing something that's low value. High value means high return. Low value — low return.

That means if you're creating a product or a service, or you're writing a book, or you're performing at a concert, or whatever your line of work is that has to have big influence on a large number of people. The more people you can influence with your work, and the more powerful your work is, the more people love your work, the more remarkable your work is, the more chances you have of generating that massive value you need in order to charge people enough of money to be getting millions of dollars back in return.

This is a tried and true principle of wealth and wealth building. Value equals wealth. What are you putting out, as far as value into the marketplace?

Either way, as a millionaire, your eye is always going to be on value. How do you create more value for the world? How do you create more value for a customer base, for your fan base? That's what you've got to work towards. That's what you have to think about when you're an entrepreneur.

Those are the fundamentals. These are the rock solid fundamentals to becoming a millionaire. You're not going to get there through some sort of lucrative investment, lucky investment, some secret stock tip or winning some lottery.

If you're very serious about becoming a millionaire, then you have to adopt all these ideas that I've told you. You have to go out and find even more. I'm just barely scratching the surface. You have to take this, you have to embody it, you have to 'start to live it. You have to start to work on yourself and transition yourself out of your job into a business.

For me, it's all the above. I want it all. How do you actually do that? To do that, you have to start to master your mind and your psychology. We got into a little bit of it here, but there's a lot more. What I found is really important is to baby-step the process. You need to be constantly working on yourself, especially as a millionaire.

We talked a lot about personal growth. You need to be constantly growing and pushing your boundaries, so that you're growing as a person. You need to become a bigger and bigger person, so you can take on more responsibility, create more value for the world. Then, you're going to get that value paid back to you over and over again.

**If You finished this book and found some value, I would love to hear Your thoughts in reviews section.**

**Also if You are interested in personal growth, feel free to take a look at my other books from this series!**